Naked Feet
Leadership

REAL PEOPLE LEADING IN
EXTRAORDINARY WAYS

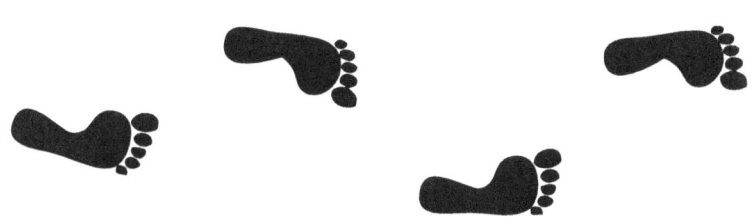

Lisa Shasky and
Cyndi Streid

Other books by these authors:
Naked Feet Living: Finding Your Real Self at Work and in Life

Visit us on our website: nakedfeetliving.com

You can also find us on Facebook/Naked Feet Book Series

ISBN: 1496122526
ISBN-13: 9781496122520

Table of Contents

INTRODUCTION

> You are not on this earth simply to do a job,
> make money, acquire things, and play a role
> that others expect of you. . . . You are here to
> be yourself and to share your real self with oth-
> ers, creating an environment . . . more in line
> with your naked feet state of mind.
> —from *Naked Feet Living: Finding Your Real
> Self at Work and in Life*

So why "Naked Feet Leadership"? Let's start with naked feet. What does this image make you think of? It might be the tickling sensation of soft, green blades of grass on the soles of your feet when you walk across your lawn, or the feel of sand massaging your feet as you leisurely stroll down the beach. Maybe wiggling your toes with a big sigh after you take your shoes off, or the pampering of a pedicure.

Now contrast those feelings with tight shoes, cramped toes, and a long day on your feet. Do you feel the difference in your thoughts, feelings, and facial expression? Which of these two mindsets—naked feet or tight shoes—is more like how you really want to be? Which is more like how you picture a "leader"?

Sometimes we put leaders and the concept of leadership on a pedestal, thinking that leaders have to be and act a certain way that's probably closer to "tight shoes" than it is to "naked feet." The truth is that leadership should be an expression of who you are on the inside—an authentic, real person, not someone who stands on a pedestal for others to admire.

What do real leaders look like, and where do they work? Do they wear suits and work in an office, or do they travel by bus to a job on a production line? Being a leader isn't about your title, role, where you live, or your income—it's about who you are and how you live your life. It's about your character, your awareness of your strengths and limitations, and your ability to inspire. Real leaders in any environment, including in a family or community, are those who act the same way in public and in private.

All Vicki ever wanted to do was be a teacher. She was thrilled to land her dream job teaching first graders. She loved seeing the joy on their faces when they completed a lesson or learned something new. She spent countless hours working on lesson plans and creating posters, always trying to do her best to teach "her kids" in new and creative ways.

Teachers take on many roles—mother, nurse, role model, psychologist, and teacher—all rolled into one job. They work long hours, not only in the classroom but also grading papers, creating lesson plans, and preparing for parent-teacher conferences in the evenings. They help prepare the rest of us to lead successful lives as parents, public servants, architects, doctors, and business owners. However, teachers don't get a lot of accolades and generally aren't mentioned in a list of top leaders.

So why are we talking about teachers in a book about leadership? On one particular morning, Vicki went to the school library to find the perfect book for her students. A short time later, she was with her students in their classroom when she heard gunshots. She hurried the kids into a closet and used her body to shield them. Victoria Soto was shot and killed protecting her students that day at Sandy Hook Elementary School. She has been recognized as a hero.

This book is about real people, living real lives, and how they choose to lead themselves and others. Some of them are heroes like Vicki Soto. She was a leader well before that fateful day. She led in how she chose to live her life, care for her friends and family, and focus on helping her kids be their best. Most leaders are not heroes, they're just regular people. They are hairdressers, fitness coaches, community volunteers, handymen, parents, secretaries, and business professionals. They struggle to pay their bills, battle health issues, and lack self-confidence. Leaders are regular people just like you and me.

Being a real leader is not about your income or being the next president. It's not a race to become the best or the biggest. *It's about becoming the best you can be and inspiring others by how you live, conduct yourself, and interact with those around you.*

Our hope is that you'll read this book with a good friend, a mentor, a close coworker, or someone else whom you trust and feel comfortable with. We recommend that you read and discuss one chapter per session. The questions at the end of each chapter (called "Getting Naked") are meant to be talked about and explored, leading you down a path of self-discovery and new ideas. You don't have to answer every question—pick the ones that apply to where you are in your life right now or that most challenge you. Feel free to probe, ask your own follow-up questions, and encourage each other to go deeper. You'll both learn more in the process.

In the pages that follow are stories of real people who made and continue to make the choice to become their best. Leadership is not a "once and done" phenomenon; it's a journey with leaps of faith, right steps, and missteps. Learning from the steps taken, these people share their journey to becoming leaders that others want to follow. Settle into your chair, kick your shoes off, and enjoy the journey of *Naked Feet Leadership!*

CHAPTER 1

THREE CS OF LEADERSHIP

I will never forget the day I made the decision that would send me into my greatest leadership role yet. I remember the moment so well because I was literally sick to my stomach thinking about facing my fear and going for it. I had been building a passionate belief for a few years but had been too afraid to share it with others. On this day, I decided to change all that.

You see, my passionate belief goes against the norm. In fact, it is one of the most controversial subjects among parents and pediatricians today. I educate parents on the risks and ingredients in vaccines. Big, hairy, controversial topic, right? This is probably one of the most important decisions a parent will make, and I decided to speak up about what I had seen and learned.

I don't know if I was consciously choosing to be a leader that day. I know it was not my intention to speak around the United States as I do now. I just wanted to share what I had learned about keeping children safe and well. I knew in my heart that other parents had a right to know this information. I was so afraid to speak out against "science," Big Pharma, and the norm, but I could no longer keep what I had learned to myself.

So in that moment, I realized it was time, no matter the cost. I was done being quiet. I was done talking to parents who stated, "I had a normally developing child until . . ." They all had similar stories of a particular day or a particular shot after which their child was never the same. How dare I keep these stories to myself? These families deserved to have a voice and let other parents know the risks and possibilities. If a mom knew I was doing something that could harm my child, I would want her to tell me. How could I sit quiet? I couldn't.

As you can imagine, that was a scary day for me, but it was also one of the most empowering and freeing days of my life. That day set me on a whole new path of living my truth. It brought me new friends, colleagues, and opportunities to help more families than I could have ever imagined. It was quite a process, but such a fun and enlightening one.

What excites me about leadership is that I believe we are all leaders in our own lives, each and every day. With your actions and your words, you are leading people. You might be leading a small army of two little ones while they watch your every move. You might lead a group of friends or colleagues who come to you for advice, or maybe it is hundreds of thousands of people that you lead. The truth is we are all leading people in our own way and on so many levels. It is really a matter of whether you are leading them intentionally or passively and whether you are leading them into your fear or your values. With each encounter, you have that choice, just like I did on that fateful day.

When studying our greatest leaders, I found there are really just a few key ingredients. Leaders come from all walks of life, but they all share a few things that I call the 3 Cs.

Cause

The first C stands for *cause*. What is your cause? In other words, what are your values? What is important to you?

These questions are huge for me. I am the kind of girl who has always been passionate about causes. Every time I watched Oprah's show, I would not sleep that night, because I was always trying to find a way to save the people featured on that episode. How could I get halfway around the world tomorrow and save those poor people? I needed to make this happen. Then the next night, it would be some other cause I wanted to be a part of. I wanted to save everybody. What I finally realized is that I could not save the world, but I could do my part. I could focus on my calling. I could focus on my cause.

We all have it, right? Something that keeps you awake at night? So the question is, what gets you really jazzed? Maybe it is having access to healthy, organic foods. Maybe it is recycling. Maybe, like me, you just want to help children express their full potential. What is your cause?

What I know is that the success of a leader is directly proportionate to that leader's passion and enthusiasm. The more passionate you are with your audience, the more impact you will have. So it is worth the time to find what you are really passionate about.

There is an exercise that I love to do when I am ready to grow to the next level of leadership. I get a pen and paper and set a timer for five minutes, and then I just write. I do not lift my pen. I just write down everything that is important to me in that moment, in my family life, my professional life, and my social life. What makes me feel super energized when I think about it? Conversely, what makes me feel very angry when I think about it? Those are the things I am passionate about. Those are my "causes." So try it. Take five minutes to just write nonstop and see what shows up.

Did you do it? Is there a pattern or a theme? This is *your* cause, and the more clear you can get about it, the more effective you will be as a leader. You need to be laser focused on your cause. We all have many things in our lives that are important to us, but what is your true calling, your true, passionate cause?

Now, once you have your cause outlined, you can take it a step further. When you are accomplishing your cause, what does it look like? What does it feel like? Write it all down in vivid detail. Really see each outcome as if it has already happened. It is so fun and so powerful to see something as if you have already accomplished it. See yourself doing it. What are you wearing? What are you saying? What are you feeling? See the people surrounding you being led by your passion and your clarity. What do they look like? Are they sitting in awe of your message? I visualize parents who are just looking for answers finding one of my posts and their prayers being answered. Just typing that gets me jazzed up!

Now, what is awesome is that the more jazzed about your cause you are, the faster you will attract and create it. I recommend you write down what you visualized and rewrite it and get more bold each time. You will limit yourself in the first few writings because of past limiting beliefs and fear, so just keep at it and get more and more grand each time. This cause has to be BIG! To be an effective leader, you have to have a clear cause and really know why that cause is so important to you. This cause will be your fuel. This cause is what will keep you full of joy and energy in your leadership.

Courage

Courage is crucial to being an effective leader. I had a huge cause building in me for a few years, but I was too afraid to share it, so I was not being a leader until I had the courage to speak out.

A great way I found to drop the fear is to really take a look at what scares you. If you became the leader you hoped to be today, what is the worst thing that could happen? Write down all the negative things that could happen. Doing this felt weird to me because I do not normally live in that space. I ultimately believe the Universe is constantly working for my greater good, but I could feel there was something there, so I had to look at it. I mean really look at it. So I just got ridiculous. I wrote down everything I could think of that could happen so I could release it for good.

I will not take up your time to list all my fears, but it turned out there were many. The more I wrote, the more showed up. I was afraid my community would think I was crazy. I was afraid my kids would be ostracized for being different. I was afraid if I told my truth, I would alienate myself and lose my income and not be able to care for my children. I was afraid of public speaking. I was afraid I would not have all the answers. Conversely, I was afraid that if I became really successful, I would lose my current circle of friends or I would be so busy, I would not have enough time with my kids.

Once I got all my fears on paper, I could really look at them for what they were. I realized that some were flat-out silly. Others were either not likely or really not that scary at all. After I got them all in front of me, it was much easier to release them and move forward.

I also realized that I was making this cause about *me*. I was worried about how people would perceive me personally, and I had to let that go. I realized that to be a great leader, you have to leave your ego at the door. Leading people is not about everyone liking you. Leadership is about telling your truth passionately and authentically.

So take the time to be honest with yourself and just get it all out on the table. What are you afraid of? What is really holding you back?

By the way, none of those things I feared have happened. Have I had people strongly disagree with me? Oh, yes! Have my children had to answer questions from their friends and teachers about some of our choices? Yes! But you know what, those experiences have made us all stronger in our belief systems and our character, so I would not change a thing. In fact, what I found is the more courageous and authentic I was about my cause, the bigger the audience became. In fact, it grew exponentially.

Commitment

Think of great leaders like Mother Teresa, Martin Luther King, and Oprah Winfrey. They worked tirelessly and fearlessly for years and years. That is not to say they were never tired or afraid. But their commitment to their causes kept them going day after day, step after step.

I believe your commitment is directly related to your cause. True leaders are dedicated and full of passion for their cause. Their cause fuels them into the wee hours of the night, on the weekends, and when they are tired. The good news is that if you know your cause, commitment is a whole lot easier. The other good news is that staying committed takes only a few fun, daily action steps.

The first thing I do each morning is write out my commitments for the day. What do I, no matter what, commit to do today before I go to sleep? I have to write down three commitments before I get out of bed. These are not things I would *like* to get done today. They are things I *will* do today. So be bold in your daily commitments, but also make them attainable. Nothing can squash a leader's motivation more than never accomplishing daily commitments. Any great success is really just an accumulation of small baby steps done each and every day.

Another commitment skill is daily affirmations. I learned about them from one of my mentors, Dr. Larry Markson. Using daily affirmations has changed my life in every aspect, including becoming the leader I aspired to be.

Basically, here's how it works: Write down statements that describe all that you want to be and do, and then say them out loud to yourself several times per day. The key is to write your statements in present tense, not future tense. For example, instead of writing and saying "I will be fit and full of energy," write and say aloud, "I AM fit and full of energy." , Just like in writing out your cause, you are seeing what you strive for as if it already exists. Here are a few more examples:

- I am confident and secure in my leadership skills.
- I deliver my message with ease and love.
- I am surrounded by a loving and service-driven team that shares my mission of raising healthy children in our world.
- The Universe is always working for me and my greater good.

Have fun with your affirmations, and say them with conviction each day, several times per day. I redo my affirmations each week and put them on my bathroom mirror, in my car, and at my desk. This way I am constantly reminded of my cause and the leader I want to be. This technique is empowering and will raise my vibration instantly. I just love it, and I know you will too!

Get Ready

So there you have it—the 3 Cs of leadership. Taking these simple steps will bring huge results. First, find your cause and see it happening in high definition. Next, face your fears and find the courage to be that leader you wish to be. Lastly, on a daily basis, write down the tasks you commit to that day and say your affirmations to keep you moving forward and growing. Your life has been waiting for its leader. Are you ready?

GETTING NAKED

1. What is your cause? Describe it in great detail.

2. Do you have the courage to follow your cause? If so, what are you currently courageously doing to follow your cause? If not, when and how will you get aligned to your cause?

3. Do you have the courage to lead in your cause? If so, how are you courageously leading in a cause you are passionate about? If not, will you? By when?

4. What three things do you commit to accomplishing today, no matter what?

5. What affirmations have you used and how have they helped you?

CHAPTER 2

FIND YOUR MOTIVATION

For me, motivation seems as natural as breathing. Growing up, I was involved in a variety of sports. I worked hard to excel in them and to achieve goals such as conference championships, personal recognition, and team success. More recently, my inner drive to be the best helped me rise through the leadership ranks in my company fairly quickly. I built a reputation for being a go-to person for starting up new operations. My philosophy can be summed up this way: Do my job successfully, and the company will be successful. When I contribute to the company's success, I will be rewarded with higher pay and more job security, allowing me to retire comfortably. It was a quick, simple, and to this date, very successful approach to my career.

In my limited leadership experience, I thought everyone was similarly motivated. Looking back, I smile at my naïveté. But thankfully, I've learned that acquiring motivation is very individualized, specific to the person and the factors that drive his or her behavior.

Let me tell you about a time in my leadership journey when this became very clear. I was assigned to start up a new call center at the large, regional real estate firm I worked for as a district manager. Like any start-up, this one offered plenty of promotional opportunities for employees who excel in their roles. This operation was a significant focus of our company, with lots of growth anticipated, and employees were carefully selected for their prior work performance and expertise. In this environment, lack of motivation seemed not only irrelevant, but an impossibility—until I encountered Sarah.

Sarah was an experienced call center employee from another department of the company. The hiring supervisor knew Sarah, since they had both worked in the same department. She was known to be a solid producer and great with customers, but her attendance was unreliable. Despite this, my supervisor believed in her; he thought a change of environment would be the boost Sarah needed to live up to her full potential. His belief in Sarah and the potential he saw for her was easy to support, so I agreed with his hiring decision, and Sarah was in our first class of new hires to our operation.

It was a great beginning for Sarah. She was a class leader throughout the eight-week training course, openly sharing her knowledge of the company's culture and performing well as she learned the new business in which she would serve our customers. She was a great example for our new hires, just as we had counted on her to be.

However, once Sarah was out of training, things began to change. Her work product was solid, but her absenteeism became noticeable. When she did come to work, she arrived late and took longer breaks and lunches than what was standard policy.

Eventually, her supervisor came to me at his wits' end. He had been trying to understand Sarah well enough to positively impact her behavior, but was having little luck. He told me he had tried everything. He had explained to Sarah that her tardiness was not acceptable, she could not be relied on, and she was letting her teammates and our customers down by not being there to take calls. She had completely exhausted her paid time-off benefits, and the supervisor was at the point of having to document her actions and his conversations with her in preparation for termination. He was visibly torn, since Sarah was the single mother of three children and he was concerned for their well-being if she were to lose her job. He asked me to have a conversation with her in hopes of a different outcome. Frankly, I wasn't sure I could do anything, given the history of Sarah's behavior. But in spite of my reservations, I scheduled a meeting with her.

At our scheduled meeting time, Sarah shuffled into my office somewhat meekly. She settled into a chair with an air of indifference and "shields up." She wore a look of defeat before a word was even said. This demeanor was in direct contrast to the woman I had seen and heard handle our customers so confidently and empathetically. I was immediately perplexed.

I asked Sarah if she knew why we were meeting. She responded yes, we were meeting to talk about her attendance. I said we did need to discuss that, but before we did, I wanted a little time to get to know her better. Sarah's eyes shot to the door, and I could sense her discomfort immediately. To put her at ease, I said, "Let me go first." I told her what I knew of her work history with our company. Then I said she was the mother to three kids: a nine-year-old son and three-year-old twins. When I mentioned her kids, she seemed to soften a bit, so I stayed on this topic. I asked her to tell me their names, where her nine-year-old went to school, his favorite topics, and the differences she noticed in the twins. She actually straightened up in her chair, leaning forward a bit and talking freely and energetically with a smile. It was easy to tell that her kids were the center of her world; she just lit up!

As we talked, I told Sarah that I could see her kids were very important to her. "They're the reason I come to work," she said. I asked her to tell me why. She talked about wanting to provide for them. She wanted to move out of government subsidized housing into a home in a safe neighborhood. She wanted to keep her kids in school and make sure they went to college. I wish I could say it was planned on my part, but in just taking the time to get to know Sarah a little better, I now saw a chance to make an impact on her attendance.

It was Sarah's turn to look perplexed when I mentioned her attendance at this job could greatly impact her children's future. I explained that being on time and taking the allotted time for breaks and lunches were important factors in the annual performance review process. She was already performing the key functions of the job well, unlike some of the other workers. If she arrived on time and worked full days, her annual performance reviews would improve, and the associated pay increases would then allow her dreams for her children to become reality.

I could see a change in Sarah's demeanor; a light was turning on. She was beginning to see a way to provide for her kids in the way she wanted.

I continued to paint a picture of Sarah's new future. I talked about how her kids would notice her efforts to get to work on time. They might not understand it right away, but over time, they would appreciate her determination to care for their needs and their future. From her example, they would learn the importance of being on time for the school bus and other activities.

I also talked about how things might be at the office. Coworkers would know they could count on Sarah to be there. She would be sought out for assistance. As she helped customers, her conversations would be overheard by those around her, making them better employees. She would be a leader among her peers.

I could see Sarah was beginning to envision this future for herself. However, I knew she wasn't totally convinced when she asked, "I can really have all of this just by being on time?" I told her that based on what I saw of her work, she was the kind of employee I wanted talking to our customers. If she continued to provide this level of service while working full shifts, she would be in the driver's seat of providing the type of future she wanted for her kids. She actually smiled one of those rare, natural smiles full of relief and possibility at the same time. It was a memorable moment.

I don't know what it took for Sarah to manage her household to get to work on time, but she figured it out. We never talked again in a formal meeting setting, but I regularly stopped by her desk to ask about the kids and their activities. It always made my day to see her face light up when she told me about the latest antics of her brood. I could readily see the difference our earlier conversation had made for Sarah, and it definitely gave me a better understanding of motivation in the workplace.

Seven years later, I ran into Sarah one night at a local convenience store. By this time, I had left the real estate firm and was working for another organization. She was standing in line with one of her sons, and we had a pleasant exchange catching up on work life and the kids' activities. She let me know she and her family now lived around the corner from the store, in a neighborhood I knew was not subsidized housing. As far as work went, she was now handling the most complex customer situations in her department and had received several promotions a long the way.

Talk about a success story! Here was a person who had good skills and had shown the ability to excel in her work, yet found herself drifting and in danger of losing her job. All she needed was to connect with the "why" behind her work.

For some of us, motivation comes from the enjoyment of the work itself or the desire to achieve certain financial or career goals. For others, it might come from the desire to provide for our families or complete challenging projects. Each person has unique skills, abilities, experiences, and desires. The truly skilled leader takes the time to look beneath the surface and help those individuals discover their motivation.

GETTING NAKED

1. What motivates you in life? In your work?

2. How does your motivation inspire you?

3. Are the actions you take aligned to what motivates you? If so, how? If not, why not?

4. Do you know what motivates your coworkers? Staff? Family members? List three people and what motivates them.

5. List three people whom, if you knew their motivation, you could positively impact.

6. Based on the positive impact you envision for the people you listed above, will you take the time to discover their motivations? If so, by when?

CHAPTER 3

LEADERSHIP IN UNEXPECTED PLACES

L eaders come in all shapes and sizes. They might even be behind you in age, rank, or "position." But these unexpected leaders can teach you some amazing lessons if you're willing to watch and listen.

Take, for example, Eli Suggs. In 2012 Eli was a typical twelve-year-old boy who liked drawing, video games, and Legos. He was a Boy Scout, attended school dances, and didn't like to read. Doesn't that sound like lots of boys his age? What isn't typical is that Eli has autism. Throughout his young life he has struggled to communicate, to interact socially, to make friends, and to be seen as "normal."

When all the students in his class at Pinetree Community School in Canyon Country, California, were invited to prepare a speech and audition to speak at their sixth grade graduation ceremony, Eli took up the challenge. He was selected to give his speech on the subject of having autism. Here's an excerpt:

You [my classmates] did not bully me. You did not make fun of me. You accepted me for who I am, just as I accepted all of you for who you are. Because of your help and friendship, I am proof that YOU—all of you—can make a difference in someone's life. I hope that I have made a difference in all of your lives too.

As we leave here today, I have a challenge for all of you. We are all different. Not less, just different. We all have things we're good at, things we need to work on and things we need help with. Whenever you see someone else who is different, instead of judging them or being a bully, I challenge you to offer help and treat that person with the kindness you have shown me these last six years. Remember, YOU—all of you—can make a difference in someone's life. You've already made a difference in mine.[1]

Wise beyond his years, Eli reminds us that each one of us has the ability to make a difference in the lives of those around us. It may seem like a small, insignificant thing at the time—like smiling at a kid who's a little different, or simply treating someone with kindness rather than judgment. If we each tried to do what he asked, what a different world this could be.

Perhaps you've heard the story of the boy who was standing on the beach throwing one starfish after another

---

1   Speech given by Eli Suggs, June 15, 2012, quoted by permission of Shannon Rosenberg, mother of Eli Suggs.

back into the ocean. When asked why he was doing this, he replied that if he didn't, the starfish would die. After it was pointed out that starfish had washed ashore on many miles of beach and that throwing back only a few of them couldn't possibly make a difference, the boy leaned down, picked up another starfish, threw it gently back into the ocean, and said, "I made a difference for that one." This powerful story, like Eli's speech, reminds us of the power in each of us to make a difference in the lives around us—that no matter how large the issues or how small we feel, we *can* make a difference, one person at a time.

Here's an example of another "starfish thrower." Imagine being a young girl, eager to go to school to learn as much as possible about the world around you, but you live in a country where girls are banned from attending school. Imagine going to school in secret, hiding from the Taliban so you can learn to read and write. You go on to write a blog describing your life, and eventually you start giving print and television interviews promoting the value of education for girls. Then one day, Taliban gunmen stop your school bus and shoot you in the head at close range. Malala Yousafzai was just fifteen years old when she was shot. Fortunately, she survived and continues to advocate for worldwide access to education.

In July 2013, Malala celebrated her sixteenth birthday by giving a passionate speech at the United Nations to emphasize that education is the only way to change lives. Imagine this tiny, soft-spoken girl, wrapped in a white shawl and pink headscarf, speaking in front of over five hundred youth and world leaders from around the world.

So here I stand, one girl among many. I speak not for myself, but so those without a voice can be heard. . . .

I am here to speak for the right of education for every child. . . .

We call upon all communities to be tolerant, to reject prejudice based on caste, creed, sect, color, religion or agenda to ensure freedom and equality for women so they can flourish. We cannot all succeed when half of us are held back. . . .

So let us wage a glorious struggle against illiteracy, poverty and terrorism, let us pick up our books and pens, they are the most powerful weapons. One child, one teacher, one book and one pen can change the world.[2]

If you haven't heard this speech, I encourage you to find it on the Internet and watch her deliver her message. Remember that this is a sixteen-year-old girl, and imagine her courage and determination to make a difference. We can learn many lessons from Malala, but here are a few that stand out to me:

- *Speak up.* You have important thoughts and ideas to share, and if you don't speak up, who will? Avoid the temptation to talk just to hear your own voice. Make sure you're coming from a place of truly wanting to make a difference,

---

2 Malala Yousafzai, speech delivered at United Nations, July 12, 2013, as transcribed at *The Independent* website, http://www.independent.co.uk/news/world/asia/8706606.html.

not just wanting to talk for selfish reasons, for personal gain, or to please others. People can spot insincerity quickly, so be sure you have no hidden agendas. Simply share your message clearly and passionately.

- *Choose your words carefully.* Words are important. They have the power to hurt, to inflame, and to cause destruction, just as they have the power to heal, to inspire, and to be constructive. In her speech, Malala said she wishes the terrorists who attacked her no harm. She went on to speak with grace and compassion about the need to ensure that every child has the right to go to school—even the children of the terrorists who tried to kill her.

- *Look beyond the immediate situation.* Malala could have focused only on her personal situation, but instead she chose to look at the bigger picture. Many people probably told her to be quiet and not attract attention. They probably warned her of the dangers and told her that her goals were impossible. Yet she looked beyond all of the dangers and dared to dream big. She doesn't see her dream of education for everyone as too large, too unrealistic, or impossible. She sees it as right.

- *Inspire others to action.* Leaders don't just point out the problem, they take action. They also ask others to take action, and they do it in a way that helps people believe they can do more than they think they can. They help others see possibilities in themselves. In her speech, Malala pointed out many specific actions that need to be taken. She wrapped it up by reminding everyone that "one child, one teacher, one book and one pen can change the world." Sometimes we need to be reminded that we've examined the problem long enough and it's time to *do something*. You will inspire others by the consistency they see and hear between your actions and your words.

Besides their young age and their courage to speak when many others, much older and allegedly wiser, would have chosen to stay silent, Eli and Malala share another trait in common. They see everyone as equal and deserving of the same rights: to get an education, to live in peace, to make friends.

These two unexpected leaders are unassuming in their day-to-day lives, but they chose to step up and speak out. Nothing about them screams "pay attention me"—just the opposite. If you passed them on the street, you might not even notice them. But instead of sitting on the sidelines and saying nothing, they each saw an inequality and chose to be the person to speak.

Leadership is not about taking the easy way out; it requires willingness to be uncomfortable, to stand up and say what you think is right. Eli and Malala shared, very clearly and succinctly, what their vision is and what we all need to do to achieve it. Sometimes it's an unexpected voice that speaks and allows the rest of us to see the world and ourselves a little more clearly.

GETTING NAKED

1. Are you a "starfish thrower"? If so, name one to three examples of how you make a difference for others. In what other areas would you like to make a difference?

2. Are you more like the person who asked why the boy was throwing the starfish? If so, what can you do differently to be more like the starfish thrower?

3. We each have something unique to offer the world. What's your gift? How will you use it to make a difference?

4. What needs do you recognize in the world around you that need a voice? How will you choose to speak up?

5. What questions do you ask yourself that empower you to consider the deeper meaning of a situation or problem? When have you been willing to change your own mind?

6. Who are the unexpected leaders in your life? What are you learning from them?

7. Are you an unexpected leader? If so, what is your message and how are you sharing it?

CHAPTER 4

GET YOUR HANDS DIRTY

Ronnie's dad taught him how do a lot of things—install windows, roofing, siding, electrical work, and plumbing; lay concrete and brick; work in the fields on the family farm; repair engines of all kinds; and much more. His dad worked hard his whole life and taught Ronnie to do the same.

At age sixteen, Ronnie drove his pickup truck from Illinois to West Virginia to visit his brother. He asked around until he found work in a logging camp as a tree topper for fifty dollars per day. He'd work wherever he could to earn ten or twenty dollars, regardless of the type of work. One day he'd do plumbing, and the next day he'd cut tobacco, do general handyman work, or clean up after a storm—you name it, he'd do it. At one point he was driving his truck through an area that was badly damaged in a flood and found people standing by the side of the road, waving twenty-dollar bills to get people to stop and help them. Ronnie even helped an elderly woman who needed him to pull a dead rat out of her crawl space.

Ronnie's philosophy is "All work is good work," and he's not afraid to get his hands dirty. In fact, he jokes that he can't get them clean. His can-do attitude explains why he always has work, when many of his friends struggle and complain there's no work out there. Ronnie is not afraid to ask anyone if there's something he can do for them, and he'll take on anything.

When I met Ronnie, he was cutting huge mountains of fallen trees into firewood with a chain saw. It looked a little like trying to bail out the ocean with a teaspoon. The entire time we loaded the firewood into my car, he was sharing the various kinds of work he'd done and looking for more ways to help me. And this was just his "side job"—he was also working as a diesel mechanic and a landscaper.

Ronnie proudly describes himself as a "jack of all trades and master of all." He takes tremendous pride in the work he does and in doing the very best quality work possible, regardless of the circumstances. Take, for example, when he worked in a coal mine, fifteen hundred feet underground. He was a "green hat"—a new miner who didn't know anything about coal mining. They start new miners out on the hardest manual labor job in the mines: working the belt line—the conveyor belt system used to move raw, unprocessed coal that is dug out from deeper in the mine. Ronnie had to walk the catwalk next to the belt line, and using a large coal shovel, he had to separate the raw bone coal (garbage) from chunk coal (the good stuff) and shovel the chunk coal onto the conveyor belt that carried it out of the mine.

On his third day on the job, Ronnie had just finished a ten-hour day and had volunteered to stay for a second shift. Suddenly his shovel got caught on a piece of chunk coal. The coal and shovel both went up the conveyer belt and out of the mine. There was no way Ronnie could walk out of the mine to get it—he was deep in the mine, and it was pitch black and impossible to know where he'd end up. There was nothing Ronnie could do about his shovel, so he did the only thing he knew to do—picking up chunks with his bare hands and throwing them on the conveyor belt. From head to toe, he was black as coal, with only see his eyes and mouth visible.

Toward the end of his second shift, the shift supervisor came up to Ronnie and asked where his shovel was. The supervisor already knew the answer. All tools are tagged and assigned to each person at the start of the shift, so he knew that Ronnie's shovel had come out of the mine more than eight hours ago. Ronnie explained what he'd done to keep up with his work. Not only had he kept up, but his belt was picked clean of chunk coal. His supervisor handed Ronnie the black hat of an experienced miner and told him he could have whatever job he wanted in the mine. That's why Ronnie worked the belt line for only three days, when most guys worked it for five or six months.

Even after he got his black hat, Ronnie didn't rest on his laurels and kick back. He took on nearly every job in the mine. He learned each of them until he could train someone to take his place and move on to the next job. Now that's being willing to literally "get your hands dirty"!

In all his jobs, Ronnie has had the chance to work around a lot of people. Some were customers; others were coworkers, bosses, or just observers. Sometimes he has been a lead worker or boss of sorts, but more often "just a worker." Others like working with him. He's willing to share what he knows, which makes everyone better. He gives others a chance to contribute, too. Working hard together teaches everyone about different group personalities, different habits, and how to work effectively as a team.

What makes Ronnie stand out is his capacity for hard work. Long hours don't deter him; neither does his role in the work or the people he's working with. And he doesn't view any kind of work as above or below him. A job needs to get done, and he's willing to do whatever it is. He works all the time. He's tough as nails, always making things, doing things, and fixing things. Every day. Even then, he still gets home before his young son goes to bed so they can play for a bit. He's dog-tired, but determined to make time for his son like his dad did for him. And he's the guy who stops for a women and her two kids on the side of the road next to their broken-down car on a Sunday. He'll spend six hours of his own time to get the car towed, find the problem, and replace her alternator—for forty dollars.

Unfortunately, we all know people with a work ethic on the opposite end of the spectrum from Ronnie's, characterized by idleness, procrastination, and laziness. Sandra was a marketing assistant with a knack for flying under the radar, doing the bare minimum to get by, and passing her work to her coworkers. She often came in late and left early, and her productivity was consistently low. She could stretch a task to take as much time as possible while her coworkers picked up the slack, and then she would complain that her efforts weren't recognized or appreciated. When her coworkers or manager attempted to talk to Sandra about her performance, she was full of excuses. She blamed her coworkers for taking her work, her manager for setting expectations too high, the work environment for being distracting, and even customers for taking too much of her time.

Sandra's coworkers and several managers tried to help her, thinking maybe she needed more training, better organizational skills, a performance improvement plan, or just extra encouragement. None of those strategies succeeded, because Sandra didn't really want to work any harder or improve.

Fortunately, we can learn just as much from someone like Sandra as we can from Ronnie. There are several things you can do to build a strong work ethic:

- *Decide what kind of impression you want to make.* Do you want to be someone your coworkers and boss can count on to pull your share of the load and step up when the chips are down? Or do you want to be the office "slacker" with a sense of entitlement? Many people view work as something to be escaped from on the weekend, to be complained about over drinks with friends, and to be dreaded as Monday rolls around. Choose instead to take initiative whenever possible, and look for problems you can help solve. You might surprise yourself and actually enjoy what you do!

- *Adopt a positive attitude.* Anger and frustration make it difficult to be at your best. Don't let your own performance start to slip while you spend your time being annoyed about others' performance. It's easy to let their behaviors rub off on you, but resist the temptation. Just because they "get away with" long lunches, frequent breaks, chatting on personal calls, or texting, that doesn't mean those behaviors are the right thing to do. Tune them out and focus on what you need to do.

- *Act on opportunity.* Thomas Edison supposedly said, "Opportunity is missed by most people because it is dressed in overalls and looks like work." That explains why many people stay stuck and don't follow their dreams or achieve their goals. Too often, people who lack a strong work ethic fail to act time and time again, and eventually they realize the world is passing them by. Learn to recognize opportunity and act on it. Knowing that you worked hard and did your best brings a sense of accomplishment that enhances overall self-worth and leads to more opportunities.

- *Develop your skills.* We're often tempted to think that successful people, like professional athletes, musicians, business owners, or others we look up to, are born with a special ability that launched them to success. However, these people will tell you they worked very hard to learn the basics and then refine their skills. And they don't stop there. They keep looking for ways to get better and new skills to add to their repertoire. They constantly push themselves to be the best they can be.

- *Maintain a balance.* Building balance in your life by having clear priorities helps you keep a healthy perspective about work. It's important to relax, recharge, and take care of yourself. This includes getting enough rest, eating healthfully, spending quality time with family and friends, and getting regular exercise.

Maya Angelou said, "Nothing will work unless you do." This statement really rings true when you think of someone like Ronnie. Successful people in all walks of life take responsibility for their own success, work hard, stretch out of their comfort zones to try new things, and experience the sense of satisfaction that comes from a job well done.

GETTING NAKED

1. Margaret Mead has been quoted as saying, "I learned the value of hard work by working hard." Are you a hard worker? How do you know?

2. How do you acknowledge the people around you who work hard? Are you recognizing and rewarding them for their hard work, or are you taking advantage of them (for example, by piling on more work or by considering them "too valuable" to move to higher positions)?

3. If you are the hard worker being taken advantage of, what can you do to change this in a positive way?

4. Are there certain kinds of work you aren't willing to do? Why or why not?

5. What benefits do you gain personally from working hard? What have you learned from working hard or from realizing you didn't give something your best work?

6. How has your work ethic paid off in your life?

CHAPTER 5

BE VISIBLE IN A CRISIS

One thousand feet in the air, the pilot and copilot suddenly felt their helicopter shudder abnormally. Steve, the copilot, looked into the eyes of the pilot. They both knew they were in trouble.

Eight months into a nine-month training program for US Army helicopter pilots, they were on a routine training run when the trouble started. Without warning, the helicopter lost its rear rotor, which is needed to keep the aircraft flying straight. Without it, the helicopter started spinning in rapid circles and began to drop like a rock. The copter landed on some pine trees, but the main rotor continued spinning, chopping through the foliage. One of the trees sheared off the top of the copter. The cabin and its occupants bounced mercilessly before everything suddenly bec°ame still.

Surprised to be alive, Steve looked down to see himself covered in blood (which turned out not to be his own). Then he looked over at the pilot, who had a large head wound and was lying unconscious. Steve's training kicked in. He jumped out, ran to the other side of the helicopter to get the pilot out, and dragged him a safe distance from the wreckage. Both men miraculously survived. At just twenty years old, Steve learned that he had the ability to stay calm and think logically in a crisis.

Steve's ability to keep calm under stress and focus on what's important would serve him well in countless situations throughout his career. Steve Calvery has dedicated more than thirty-five years to his country and to public service:

- After the training accident, he went on to serve as a helicopter combat pilot in the Vietnam War, where he was wounded, nearly mortally, and was awarded a Purple Heart.
- He went into the Secret Service, where he served on the protection details of two presidents and one vice president.
- After 9/11, he was asked to develop and implement a plan to protect this country's critical infrastructure and national monuments, which he did at the Department of the Interior.
- Shortly thereafter, he took over the fledgling Pentagon Force Protection Agency (PFPA), which was created after 9/11 to defend the Pentagon from another attack.
- He sought to professionalize the PFPA, including emphasizing the importance of active shooter training. This training enabled his officers to successfully shoot and stop an active shooter who appeared at one of their entrances in 2010. If the shooter had gotten past the doors, scores of innocent people would have been killed. The officers credited their success to their recent active shooter training.

The common thread in these incidents is Steve's willingness, time and time again, to be in the line of fire (literally or figuratively). He is willing to be the "go-to" guy, a voice of calm in the midst of chaos, able to make decisions regardless of the situation.

Think of the star basketball player who wants the ball in the most critical situations, who is willing to take the potential game-winning shot and take the consequences—good or bad. This willingness to be visible and lead from the front is perhaps more important than ever in a crisis.

Another good example is the leadership of New York City mayor Rudy Giuliani in the wake of 9/11. In the midst of this immense tragedy, he was seemingly everywhere—on television, with firefighters, meeting with experts, consoling the grieving, and vowing to rebuild the city. This situation was filled with uncertainty, and the mayor sometimes didn't have all the information or answers. He could have taken shelter, kept his head down, and played it safe. But instead, he was on the scene when things were toughest, leading the charge and making the best possible decisions with the available information.

The visible leaders in a crisis seem to have several traits in common: training, anticipation, unwavering decision-making ability, emotional control, and unconditional honesty. Even if you're not in the military or Secret Service like Steve, having a high level of training is critical. Being as knowledgeable as possible in your field will give you a broad base from which to draw when solving problems or making decisions. Being well trained is something we each need to take ownership of, instead of relying on someone else to tell us what we need to know.

This training is closely tied to your ability to anticipate potential problems and solutions. You can't be prepared for all possible crises, but leaders need to have an arsenal of options and tools they can draw from when the unexpected hits. Many businesses have disaster recovery plans that they test with various potential scenarios. This testing helps them identify gaps and evaluate the strengths and weaknesses of people, processes, and technology so they can plan for whatever arises. The same principles hold true on an individual level.

One strategy that can help is to practice looking at the whole situation rather than becoming focused on one particular facet. Military personnel are taught to do this to avoid the tendency for tunnel vision.

Perhaps one of the hardest things to do is to control your emotions. Even top-notch performers and leaders can "lose it" when thrust into high-stress, chaotic, unexpected situations they are not equipped to handle. As a leader, you must be able to manage your emotions so that you maintain a sense of urgency while remaining even-tempered. People are looking at your verbal and nonverbal cues to gauge their own reactions.

Tied closely to controlling your emotions is unconditional honesty. Leaders must be able to deliver bad news in a way that prevents panic and provides a realistic level of hope for the future. You must be sensitive to how people will react to the information, yet not shy away from reality. People want the facts and to know the path forward.

Unfortunately, we've all experienced "leaders" who seem to disappear when things get tough. Maybe a new policy or reorganization isn't received well in the workplace, and the key leaders remain too busy in meetings to take time to talk to their people, listen to their concerns, and take an active role in resolving them. Or perhaps a coworker wants to be seen as a leader, but when the task is difficult and may not be successful, this person is content to sit back and critique the efforts of those who choose to get involved.

Not many people face life or death consequences in their daily lives. But being willing to step up, take responsibility, and be visible in difficult situations is important regardless of the setting or consequences.

Tim is a high-end home builder and specialty woodworker on the New Jersey shore. As a successful, highly regarded builder and businessman, he works with a large number of subcontractors on a regular basis. When the Great Recession hit and new home building ground to a halt, he turned to remodeling, repairs, and similar jobs to keep his business afloat and find work for his subcontractors. Rather than close up shop like so many others, Tim felt a deep sense of responsibility for all the workers who depended on him. He chose to fight for his own business and to keep those workers employed.

Tim continued to be as visible as possible. For example, he brought lunch to his quality subcontractors and skilled tradesmen at their work sites—even when they were working for someone else. It wasn't just about the food; it was really about maintaining the relationships. He took the time to talk with the workers, taking a sincere interest in them as people. He asked them what their challenges were, offered suggestions for finding more work, and listened to their ideas. Together, they worked to find ways to survive the downturn.

After Hurricane Sandy hit the East Coast in 2012, home building and repairs picked up dramatically. Tim was able to hire the best subcontractors and tradesmen because they realized he had been there for them when times were tough. While many other builders were focused only on themselves, Tim continued to network in the community, helping those he'd worked with in the past find or enhance their skills. He could have looked out for his own interests by moving to another area or simply closing his business, like many others did. But he felt an obligation to be there for all the workers that had helped him build his business. He has been willing and able to take on the toughest rebuilding jobs and fine woodworking and restoration projects in Sandy's aftermath.

The bottom line for both Steve and Tim is the willingness to be visible, available, and actively involved, no matter how difficult the circumstances or how they might affect them personally. Real leaders want responsibility and take personal accountability for the outcome, whether good, bad, or somewhere in between.

GETTING NAKED

1. How do you react when a situation is especially challenging or difficult? Do you tend to retreat, or do you get involved in leading toward a solution? Explain why.

2. What did Tim do that engaged and empowered those around him? How can you do this?

3. Do you tend to sugarcoat bad news, telling others what you think they want to hear? Or do you help others face the reality of the situation? How do you do this?

4. How do you inspire others to have faith and reassure them that they will prevail—that they will get through the crisis?

CHAPTER 6

BOUNCE BACK FROM ADVERSITY

Survivors are people who carry on or persevere despite hardships or trauma. Somewhere deep inside, they believe they have a choice in how they respond or what the outcome will be.

Do you remember the rock climber whose arm was pinned under an eight-hundred-pound boulder? He was hiking alone and had told no one where he was going, so he knew it was unlikely anyone would find him. He could have decided his situation was hopeless, given up, and died. Instead, he realized he had options. He tried to free his arm; he pounded away at the boulder; he tried to move it. By his own account, during his five-day ordeal he experienced the full range of emotions, from despair to optimism and back again, as he eliminated each option. Finally he was left with only one alternative: cut off his own arm. In the end, he was able to do what was necessary to survive.

Not all survivors have done something as traumatic as cutting off their own arm or surviving a natural disaster. You might not even recognize some of them as survivors at first glance.

Take Jim, for example. His professional résumé includes multiple Emmy Awards for writing, producing, and directing during a thirty-year career in commercial television. A popular and highly regarded professor at UCLA and Ball State University, he taught students who have gone on to win many Emmys of their own. The National Academy of Television Arts and Sciences honored him with a lifetime achievement award for his contributions. He and his wife have been "proctor parents" to many teenagers whose parents were in trouble with the law.

Behind all this success is the rest of the story. For most of his life, Jim felt different from everyone else—restless, unfocused, and just "off." He struggled terribly in school, rarely getting grades above a D. Teachers, other kids, and even his own mother called him "dumb" and "stupid." In an attempt to figure out was wrong with him, Jim's parents and school arranged for him to see multiple psychiatrists. He even spent time in a mental hospital on a few occasions.

Although he never graduated from high school, Jim eventually took some community and junior college classes. He managed to graduate from college and earn a master's degree. But even after he launched his career in television, he found himself easily bored, impatient, and prone to mistakes if the project was too slow or not challenging enough. The more complex projects gave him an extra rush, and he thrived in that environment.

In his mid-forties, Jim was diagnosed with attention deficit hyperactivity disorder (ADHD). He began taking Ritalin, a drug used to treat ADHD symptoms. For the first time in his life, he felt "normal."

But that was not the end of Jim's challenges. Some time later, his wife was diagnosed with Stage IV ovarian cancer and underwent multiple rounds of chemotherapy and experimental treatments. During his wife's illness, in his late fifties, Jim was diagnosed with prostate cancer and then Parkinson's disease. Not long after, his only son died unexpectedly.

Jim's story is inspiring not just because of his awards and fame, or even because of his hardships, but because of his ability to keep going. When many would have become discouraged, folded up their tent, and given up, he kept fighting—both professionally and personally.

The leadership trait that Jim exhibits—as do others who have come through difficult events in their lives—is resilience. Being resilient doesn't mean avoiding emotional pain, sadness, anger, or other "negative" emotions. It means being able to overcome adversity and keep moving forward. It's the ability to bounce back from difficulty. Resilience enables people to successfully adapt to tragedy, threats, health problems, workplace stressors, and much more.

Consider the story of John Franklin Stephens. Born with Down syndrome, during his entire life he has had to fight against others' perception that he is dumb, slow or "different." He's endured stares, patronizing behavior, taunts, teasing, and being left out. Despite these experiences, he describes his life in glowing terms—living and working in his community, having many friends, and working as a Global Messenger for Special Olympics. In this role he makes speeches all over the country, educating others on the lives of those with intellectual disabilities and the role of Special Olympics.

When a notable conservative commentator used the word "retard" to refer to President Obama, Stephens responded with an open letter to explain why he was offended. His letter was widely published and much praised. In it he wrote:

> After I saw your tweet, I realized that you just wanted to belittle the President by linking him to people like me . . . You, and society, need to learn that being compared to people like me should be considered a badge of honor. No one overcomes more than we do and still loves life so much.[3]

Stephens signed the letter "A friend you haven't made yet." Now if that isn't resilience (and grace), what is?

Becoming resilient is not a one-time event, but more like a process or journey that takes time and effort. Here are a few tips that can strengthen your resilience:

- *Know yourself and what is truly important to you.* When everything around you feels chaotic, having a sense of what your values are, what you believe in, what you are good at, and what your goals are can provide you with a sense of direction. When you don't get the job or assignment you wanted, do you blame the boss or coworkers and bemoan your bad luck, or do you take a realistic look at the situation and focus on your values, strengths, and goals?

---

3   John Franklin Stephens, "An Open Letter to Ann Coulter," posted by Tim Shriver on *The World of Special Olympics* (blog), October 23, 2012, http://specialolympicsblog.wordpress.com/2012/10/23/an-open-letter-to-ann-coulter.

The latter approach often provides some insight into other, better choices you can make. It also helps you stop the emotional swirl that often accompanies a setback and lets you view it more calmly.

- *Actively seek out those who will speak truthfully to you.* Resilient people tend to have a strong network of trusted friends, colleagues, and mentors. They can reach out to this network when they need advice or help getting back on track. Sometimes this network happens more naturally because someone has a circle of friends, coworkers, or built-in mentoring relationships that keeps them grounded and challenged. But for most of us, it takes some deliberate effort to build this network. Building a network is especially important in small businesses where there are few employees and little formal mentoring structure or culture of helping others succeed. There are countless ways to find mentors and build a network: LinkedIn, professional trade groups, your local chamber of commerce, community groups, local clubs, places of worship, volunteer opportunities, and more. The added benefit of volunteering is that helping others can shift your perspective and remind you that you are not alone; others need help also.

- *Ask questions and keep learning.* None of us knows everything, and we need to be okay with that. The world around us is complex and changing rapidly. We can't figure out everything out for ourselves, and we certainly can't do it all by ourselves. Don't fall into the trap of not asking questions because you don't want to look dumb, you're afraid to show others what you don't know, or my personal favorite—you think the other person is too busy. These are all excuses for not increasing your knowledge and learning from other people's experience. Why deprive others of the opportunity to share their knowledge with you?

- *Fail fast and move on.* It's tempting to stay in a comfort zone where you have the skills to navigate successfully. However, you'll learn more if you're willing to step out of your comfort zone. So go out on a limb and try something new, even if you fail. Today's failure is the key to tomorrow's success! The key is to evaluate what happened and learn from it. Is there anything you would do differently next time? Anything you did particularly well? As you try more and more new things, you'll gain confidence in your ability to face new and challenging circumstances. You'll be able to draw on your varied experiences to make better decisions.

- *Take time for yourself.* Healthy habits are the foundation for mental, emotional, and physical resilience. But when we find ourselves in challenging circumstances, those healthy habits are often the first things to go. We stop exercising, don't get enough sleep, make unhealthy food choices, and perhaps drink more alcohol than we should. It seems counterintuitive to take time away from the crisis of the moment to take care of yourself, but the benefit is that you'll come back more energized and better able to tackle the challenge. Research shows that taking regular mental breaks, exercising at least thirty minutes a day, eating healthy foods, and getting at least eight hours of sleep each night will help lower your stress and increase your ability to solve problems.

- *Accept that difficulty is a part of life.* Focus your energy on those things you can control. I once heard a minister say that when you don't know what else to do, just do the next faithful thing. So keep putting one foot in front of the other. Take one small step, and then the next, and then the next . . .

GETTING NAKED

1. When you think about the kinds of events that cause you the most stress or pain, what themes or common threads can you identify?

2. What impact have stressful events had on you? How did you deal with the effects (positively and negatively)?

3. What impact did your reaction to those events have on those around you, such as coworkers, bosses, friends, and family?

4. What have you learned about yourself in experiencing those events?

5. What has helped you overcome those events? How has it helped?

6. What role have friends, family, civic groups, spiritual advisers, mentors, and others played in helping you move through difficult times?

7. What would you do differently in the future when encountering challenging life events?

8. Which of the resiliency tips will you work on over the next thirty days?

CHAPTER 7

CREATE A POSITIVE ENVIRONMENT

Have you ever walked into a business and just felt from the moment you crossed the threshold that the staff enjoyed working there and wanted you to feel good for being there? The dentist's office where Jamie works as the office manager is one of those places. When you walk into that office, Jamie looks up, smiles, makes eye contact, greets you enthusiastically, and makes you feel like the most important person in the room. Lots of people are fearful or tense when they come to a dentist, but Jamie has a remarkable way of putting people at ease. She answers every question as if it's the first time she's heard it (even though it's probably the thousandth). She is always patient and kind regardless of how she's treated.

Jamie's positive attitude is shared by everyone who works there, from the office staff to the dental assistants, the hygienists, and the dentists themselves. Together they have created an atmosphere that is positive, friendly, welcoming, and enjoyable to work in. They all genuinely seem to respect and like each other. They guard this atmosphere carefully, holding each other accountable to maintain it.

Conversely, we've all experienced—whether as an employee or a customer—businesses that are just the opposite. No one looks up when you come in; it seems like a bother when you ask a question; coworkers don't get along; and you want to spend as little time there as possible. Ted worked in a place like this. His boss rarely interacted with him or other employees and didn't seem to know or care about their work. When Ted asked questions or brought up issues, his boss seemed uninterested and rarely offered direction or feedback. The boss and his coworkers spent considerable time each day bad-mouthing their customers, as well as each other, and looking for ways to do as little as possible.

I'm guessing you'd rather work with Jamie than with Ted. So how can we help create the kind of positive work environment that we all wish for? Whether or not you have a formal leadership title, there are constructive ways you can help build the kind of atmosphere you and others desire.

Be a Positive Person

Building a positive environment starts with each of us as individuals. Walk around with a smile, make eye contact, and say "Hi" to the people you pass in the halls. Go out of your way to be friendly and kind. Take a genuine interest in those around you. Resist the temptation to fall into gossip, whining, and complaining—these may seem like easy way out, but they are like weeds in your garden. They start small, and at first you really don't notice them, but pretty soon they've taken over and crowded out what you actually intended to grow.

Decide to make the most out of your work experience, even if it's not ideal. Focus on why you are there and how you can make the best of anything that comes your way. A positive attitude gives you power. With it, you can increase your job satisfaction and set the tone for yourself and those around you.

Recognize That Everyone Has Strengths

Each one of us has unique strengths, skills, goals, and dreams. If you sometimes struggle to identify these in yourself, it may help to bounce ideas off someone else. Whether it's a trusted friend, coworker, mentor, or boss, find someone who can help you articulate what your strengths are and how they do or don't fit into your goals.

Remember, goals can change throughout your life. Maybe at one point your goals and dreams were related to achieving a certain position or making a certain income. Later they may shift to having a more flexible schedule or building skills you can use in retirement. There are no bad goals—you just need to know what yours are so you can plan toward them.

If you're a boss, remember that there is no expiration date on talent. Don't discount workers just because they are older, are changing careers, or don't have the skills and strengths you are most familiar with. Help your employees see where they are today in relation to their goals. If they are lacking needed skills and experience, brainstorm how they can close the gap. Maybe they could join a mentoring group, organize a children's sports league, or lead a project at work that uses a new skill. One of the most powerful things you can do for someone is to help them use their talents and passions to achieve their goals and contribute in the workplace.

Set High Expectations and Recognize Good Work

Do you remember your favorite teacher? For me, it was Miss Slaughter, my high school anatomy teacher. She was the toughest, most demanding teacher I ever had. She set what seemed like impossibly high standards, packed more into her curriculum than any other teacher, and made us think for ourselves and work hard. What made her so great in my eyes was that she believed in each one of us. She challenged us to do our best work and demanded we treat each other with respect.

I recall one assignment I turned in. I thought it was "good enough," but Miss Slaughter pulled me aside. She told me she was disappointed in my work because she knew I was capable of doing better. She gently but firmly pointed out some areas of my paper that could be better, and then she challenged me to try again. I worked my tail off to improve that assignment. I walked away with not only an A, but the determination to never do less than my best work. I remember the look on Miss Slaughter's face and the pride in her eyes when she told me, "I knew you were capable of this kind of work!" She treated each person in her class with respect, set high expectations for us, and then helped us believe in ourselves enough to meet them.

In the workplace, showing respect and setting high (yet realistic) expectations are just as important as they were in Miss Slaughter's class. We all want to know what is expected of us. When managers are very clear about expectations and the rewards that are attached to various levels of performance, employees will be more engaged and motivated.

Recognition is also essential. Noticing when someone performs well and recognizing them for it goes a long way. When you offer recognition, be as specific as possible. Rather than a vague "good job," say exactly what quality or skill the person demonstrated. For example: "Krista, thank you for working overtime yesterday so we could finish that report. I really appreciate the extra effort and attention to detail."

Recognizing excellent performance helps employees feel valued and respected. It also fosters an environment where colleagues and leaders help each other and feel a strong sense of teamwork.

Give Yourself and Others Room to Fail

Mistakes are a natural part of learning and growing, so it's healthy to create a culture where it's okay to fail. As a leader, you need to help people feel comfortable with making mistakes, learning from them, and moving on.

Sometimes people are afraid to make mistakes, afraid to speak up, afraid to challenge others. In that atmosphere of fear, morale drops, stress increases, and productivity suffers. Most importantly, no one can do their best work in an environment like this. Fear of making mistakes is part of being human, and it shows you care about the work you're doing, but don't let yourself or others be trapped by that fear. Mistakes and failures will happen, but so what? Figure out what you learned from them and move on.

Address Negative Behavior

There are doubtless many more ways you can contribute to a positive work environment, but one more concept is important to understand: don't let one bad apple spoil the barrel. Jamie would be the first to say she isn't the only one responsible for creating the positive tone in her office. Everyone in the office plays an important role in contributing to the overall atmosphere. If something threatens to spoil that atmosphere—perhaps a coworker's negative behavior or a difficult customer—the staff members realize they have a choice. They can either let the apple continue to rot and ruin everything, or they can pick it out, address it, and thus protect the rest of the barrel.

Addressing a "bad apple" often starts with finding the source of the negative behavior so you can help without exacerbating the situation. For example, a customer may be upset about something else that happened that day or about service received somewhere else. It's often best to "kill them with kindness"—be as helpful as possible, remain positive, and do your best to let the person's negative attitude roll off your back. For coworkers, consider things like whether their workload or responsibilities have changed. Do they act similarly with all coworkers, or could there be personal stresses that are impacting them at work? Then have a private, respectful conversation. Let the person know you are concerned and explain how the negative behavior is impacting the workplace. Be supportive, but firm that the behavior needs to change. We all have bad days, but a prolonged negative attitude should be addressed for the health and productivity of everyone in the workplace.

GETTING NAKED

1. How do you show genuine interest in the people around you?

2. What can you do to help coworkers or friends identify and use their strengths?

3. What three things can you do to recognize and appreciate your coworkers or staff?

4. Why do you think we're often so afraid to make mistakes? How can you move past that fear and "fall forward"?

5. Can you apply the ideas in this chapter to your family? What can you do to create a positive environment at home?

CHAPTER 8

Find and Follow Your Passion

P am is a successful leader in the field of marketing. I met her at a professional development seminar, where she was the featured speaker. She took a humdrum event and turned it on its ear with her energy and passion. She had everyone in the room fully engaged, enthusiastically taking notes, and hanging on her every word. This woman knew how to communicate and share her passion! Later, she agreed to meet with me and share more about her life, leadership, and her passion for her work.

Pam told me about a time when she was relaxing on the beach, with her husband within arm's reach and the pleasant chemistry of her drink of choice, red wine, hitting her palate. The sky was clear, the sun warm, the breeze just right . . . the only thought coming to her mind was "Aahhh." She was very much enjoying the moment. She had been invited to this paradise location to speak to a large group of sales professionals at a convention. Of course she said yes. She was ready for a beach getaway, and she looked forward to interacting with a group of professionals she knew well and who embraced the power of marketing.

So there she was, lying on the beach with her eyes closed on the day before her presentation. Suddenly something blocked the sun, casting a shadow that caused her eyes to open with a look of "And to what do I owe this interruption?" Standing in front of her was the executive who had invited her to present to this group. He told her that instead of talking about marketing, he wanted her to talk about something outside her field of expertise—something she could relate to the leadership skills that this group was being asked to develop. Hmm, that wasn't what Pam was expecting. That was the end of her wonderful afternoon on the beach soaking up the sun, since she now had to create a new presentation to deliver in front of a large group of expectant sales professionals. No pressure there.

Actually, though, as Pam settled herself on her hotel room's balcony, a topic very near and dear to her heart came to mind. The topic was passion—passion in life; passion for people, hobbies, interests; passion for loving one's work. Bingo! Pam immediately became excited. She felt fortunate to have the opportunity to talk about the value of passion in the workplace and for the work one does for a living.

The topic of passion seemed very fitting to this audience and also to Pam herself. She lives her life by the well-known mantra put into song by one of her favorite country artists, Gretchen Wilson: "I'm here for the party and I ain't leaving 'til they throw me out." And since parties of one aren't as enjoyable as those with others, a passion for leadership is fitting when considering the workplace is also an appropriate party location. A workplace party doesn't mean loud music playing in the background, food, beverages, and multiple conversations taking place at one time. Rather, it means letting one's enjoyment for leading in the workplace shine through in actions and conversations.

Following are the highlights of Pam's passion presentation. She has used it over and over when looking beyond her field of expertise to move an audience.

• • •

"Let's start simple. What is passion? Passion is a feeling. It's that 'fight' inside you, the voice that doesn't stay quiet, that doesn't gloss over something that triggers a reaction inside you. Others may not see your passion or react in the same way you do, but you know something has changed for you internally. Something turned your head and caught your attention—maybe not in a physical way that others can see, but internally, you feel different than you did just minutes before the subject or activity was brought to your attention.

"How do you figure out what you are passionate about? It's as easy as taking a little time with yourself to determine the following. First, figure out what you enjoy. Second, check in with yourself frequently to ensure you are enjoying what you are doing. Third, don't settle for less than what inspires and energizes you. Fourth, realize that if you feel your passion subsiding, it may be time to move onto another passion.

"Passion is critical in the role of a leader. It is imperative to have a passion for what is important to those you lead. One doesn't have to look beyond employee engagement survey results to determine that many workplaces are filled with people in leadership roles that have no passion for their staff or their interests. Some people get into leadership roles in the workplace or in their lives (for example, raising children) because somewhere along the line it seemed like the 'next step' on the treadmill of life. There is no room for the treadmill when one is making life choices based on one's passions.

"Passions come in various shapes and sizes, from inspiring others to follow their dreams to shaping the youth of our world, assisting the elderly, putting a smile on the face of a stranger, designing jewelry, speaking in public, serving others—the list is limitless and undefined. For me, I know I'm passionate about making money. Some may not think this is an admirable passion, but it is my passion. It energizes me to know I am taking care of my family, surpassing the expectations of my youth, and impacting large workforces, since that is part of my role as a company executive.

"On a regular basis I sit down, usually with a glass of a favorite red wine, and reflect on what is happening in my life. Sometimes I invite my husband or close friends to join me, and other times, it's just me. The question is, 'Am I enjoying what I'm doing and what is going on in my life?' My answers have varied over the years. At times, the answer is not 'Yes,' but rather, 'Absolutely!' At other times it's 'Yes, but I would like more time with my husband and family' or 'Yes, but I want more of . . .' In these instances, I create 'next steps' that allow me to increase the quality of time spent in an area from which I get energy. If chosen appropriately, the next steps also eliminate or decrease time spent in an area I hold no passion for. And there have been times when the answer to my question is 'No.' When that happens, I come up with a plan for more activity—some may say, an overhaul of life—to get to what my passion is or is becoming. I might decide to make a career change, work on personal growth, or improve my physical health.

"These quiet moments allow me to step off the treadmill of life and refocus on what I am passionate about. And after many years, I still get surprised when a passion has run its course within me. In these moments, I realize I have choices. I can continue to do what I've been doing and lose myself in an activity or role, or I can take action toward a new passion. I happen to enjoy making a lot of money, and to fulfill that passion, I need to take certain actions. Making sure my actions are consistent with my passion has enabled me to fulfill this core passion consistently over time.

"Believe me, making time for personal reflection is not always easy to do, and sometimes the answers have truly made me uncomfortable. My discomfort has led to sleepless nights, fluffing the pillow incessantly, snapping at family and coworkers, and pouting at those most important to me. However, I have finally grasped the fact that life is short, and as much as I'm passionate about making money, I am just as passionate about getting the most out of this party called life! So I make this time, reflect honestly, and step into my passions, whether they're something I'm already doing or something I haven't tried but feel called to do. I have found that consistently including activities, people, and experiences in my life that inspire me and give me energy allows me to be the best I can be for those around me, at work and at home. Doing this, in turn, allows those people to feel free to be their best, resulting in parties of many showing up in many aspects of my life. It makes for a job worth doing, friends worth having, a life worth living!"

GETTING NAKED

1. What are you passionate about professionally? Regarding your family and friends? For you and you only?

2. For each of the passions you identified in question 1, list the amount of time (daily, weekly, or monthly) you spend on it.

3. What do you enjoy doing on the job? With family and friends? By yourself? Whom do you enjoy spending time with?

4. For the each item you identified in question 3, list the amount of time (daily, weekly, or monthly) you spend on it.

5. What *don't* you enjoy doing on the job? With family and friends? By yourself? Whom *don't* you enjoy spending time with?

6. For each item you identified in question 5, list the amount of time (daily, weekly, or monthly) you spend on it.

7. Review your lists and time commitments and identify a passion or two from your lists that you want to spend more time on. What steps will you take to do this? Name others who would benefit if you took these steps.

9. Sleep on it. Set a time to come back to this activity. Write down what passion(s) you will add to your life, what steps you will take, who will benefit, and when you will begin this journey.

CHAPTER 9

EMBRACE THE POWER OF EMPATHY

If you've spent any time practicing or learning about leadership, you are probably familiar with the concept of empathy. Sometimes misunderstood as being "touchy-feely," empathy is actually a valuable and powerful leadership skill. It gives a leader insight into what others are thinking or feeling and what their priorities and interests are. It helps you see things through someone else's eyes.

Empathy in the workplace results in staff members who feel supported, engaged, and free to contribute their own creativity. Leaders with empathy have never been more important than in this age of ever-increasing technology, mobile workers, and virtual teams. Numerous studies have linked empathy to positive business results. But what about the power of empathy when extended to a customer? When an employee is empathetic to a customer's needs, how does that affect the customer's feelings about the organization?

Let's jump back in time to the spring of 2011. An unusual number of strong tornadoes ravaged the Midwest and Southeast, devastating small towns and large cities alike.

They wreaked havoc on property, caused long-lasting physical and mental injuries, and resulted in significant loss of life.

One of the communities affected was Smithville, a small town tucked away in the northeast corner of Mississippi. It's a town where things move a little slower, everyone knows each other, and the Friday night football game is a major social event. In March 2011 a tornado tore through this small town, leaving catastrophic devastation in its wake. The majority of Smithville homes were damaged or destroyed, and fierce winds carried the high school's football scoreboard more than twenty miles away, dumping it unceremoniously in the neighboring state of Alabama.

In response to the devastation, first responders, utility crews and volunteer groups rush into the area to begin recovery efforts. Next come roofers, contractors and other disaster restoration businesses. Some of these businesses are large, highly respected companies that specialize in managing large scale recovery efforts and are dedicated to the well-being of their customers. They sent teams of technicians to Smithville to assess the damage and begin repairs, and managers, who lead and direct the work. These workers deal with devastation day after day, season after season. As a result, they are highly experienced. Unfortunately, they may also become desensitized. It's not that the managers or technicians are uncaring or unfeeling. But in order to complete their work, they must shut down a part of their emotions. This storm, though devastating to the residents of Smithville, was just another day at the office for those in the disaster recovery business.

A seasoned manager, Nick, arrived in Smithville a week after the storm to check on the team's progress. The operation was in full swing when he arrived. Nick and the onsite manager, the person responsible for day-to-day supervision of the technicians, went out to complete several field visits.

Nick noticed that the technicians were hard at work, completing their tasks efficiently and skillfully and moving from one appointment to the next as quickly as possible. However, something was missing. They were not taking the time to listen to the customers' stories and empathize with them.

Nick and the onsite manager discussed this as they were driving around. What could be possible if the technicians slowed down just a bit? What would happen if they listened to each customer as if this was the first time they had heard such a tale of destruction?

Nick called an all-staff meeting and shared the following messages:

- Remember that our business, at its core, is always about people and that the people of Smithville need us.
- Despite the possible negative impact to your workload, slow down and take the time to connect with customers when you are with them.
- Listen to customers' stories of what this tornado did, not only to their property, but to them personally. And listen as if it's the first time you've heard about such devastation.
- Allow yourself to feel empathy for the people you are trying to help. Who better to be empathetic than someone who has seen this type of destruction as often as you have?
- Allow yourself to feel pride to be there at your customers' time of need and to give them hope.

- Prioritize your workload to ensure you are going to home sites with the most significant damage before less-impacted home sites.

As work resumed, the onsite manager followed these guidelines himself and emphasized their importance to the staff. The operation started to make a dramatic impact in the community, and the technicians' workload benefitted too.

- By listening to the customers' stories first, they were avoiding rework for overlooked damage.
- By slowing down, staff were picking up on customers' nonverbal body language, which helped them understand whether more or less time was needed with a customer at the site. Staff were able to address any concerns or questions regarding the recovery and repair process, personal belongings, or how to rebuild while standing at the home site with the customer, eliminating additional calls and site visits.
- Staff became better at managing their work time. That is, they understood the value of spending an appropriate amount of time with the customer at the site, balancing this against the time they would need to spend with their other customers with whom they still had appointments.
- Staff could better understand the power of helping their customers. They saw that help might mean more than completing a repair or cleaning up after water and fire damage. Help, at times, means addressing unseen damages just by taking the time to listen to someone's story.

- Having felt heard and understood, customers started to assist in prioritizing the technicians' work. Some of them deferred their scheduled appointments to other customers that they knew had more damage.

In the end, this became a life-changing event for both customers and technicians. The technicians reconnected with their customers on a more personal level, which allowed them to work more effectively to serve the needs of the community. Customers spoke in glowing terms about the technicians who took the time to really listen to their stories about how the tornado upended their life. And the company has no doubt won many customers for life, solidifying their presence in Smithville, due to one leader's focus on empathy.

GETTING NAKED

1. When was the last time you were empathetic to an employee's situation? Explain the situation and how your empathy affected the outcomes for you, your employee, and the business or workload.

2. Describe a time when you asked an employee to be empathetic to a workplace peer or subordinate. Explain the situation and how the employee's empathy affected the

outcomes for you, your employee, the person shown empathy, and the business or workload.

3. Describe a time when you or an employee were empathetic to a customer of your company. Explain the situation and how the empathy affected the outcomes for you, your employee, the customer, and the business or workload.

4. If you cannot recall being empathetic with an employee or customer, why are you not utilizing this leadership skill? What might be possible if you were empathetic with an employee? A customer?

CHAPTER 10

Invite Others to the Conversation

I have had the opportunity to be in leadership for many years, the last few years devoted to working with other leaders to transform our organization to meet the changing needs of today's customers. It's challenging, rewarding, and stressful work. I believe my success is due in part to keeping four questions in mind when working with and leading others. These questions form the foundation of my communication in all relationships—professional and personal:

- Does it *need* to be said?
- Does it need to be said *now*?
- Does it need to be said by *me*?
- Is what I am about to say honest and kind?

Each of us has had a moment (or two or ten) when we wish we had stopped talking before we actually did stop talking. Or we may wish we had never opened our mouths at all. For me, it was right after starting a new job. Instead of having to interview for the job, I was simply asked if I wanted it. While the manner in which the position was offered was complimentary, it also generated in me a strong desire to demonstrate my value. I jumped into the team discussions with vigor, speaking my thoughts directly, bringing new ideas, and questioning existing processes. Without knowing it, I quickly earned a reputation for being pushy and self-seeking. My zealousness to prove my value had inadvertently alienated team members and made it difficult for me to connect with peers. It took months to repair the damage and build trusting relationships. It was a hard lesson, but one that led me to the four questions that have served me well since then.

Does It Need to Be Said?

Let's begin with "Does it need to be said?" The answer may seem obvious, but often it is less so than initially appears. Here are my clues to determine whether what I feel compelled to share is necessary:

- *Will the information move the discussion or project forward?* Speaking for the sake of speaking is not moving anything forward. Doing so may even take on a life of its own, especially in the context of a new venture or problem no one is quite sure how to solve. One participant may point out that the problem is difficult. Then for the next ten minutes, all parties in the room chime in saying the same basic thing. Their comments don't help solve the problem, and in fact they waste time. Don't misunderstand; I am not discounting brainstorming sessions or building affinity and identification. Rather, I am suggesting that being judicious with words is a productive habit to get into. If the point has been made, let it rest and move on.

- *Is my comment positive?* Nothing brings creativity to a standstill quite like negativity. Creativity, especially in a work setting, requires vulnerability. The act of creation, of bringing a new thought or idea forward, requires that you relax your guardedness and deliver something raw. You cannot control others' reaction to it. All you can do is bravely offer it up. On the flip side, if what you are about to say is critical or defeatist, it will discourage others from offering truly original thoughts of their own. One of the senior leaders in my organization is known for saying, "Don't tell me what you can't do; tell me what you *can* do." She understands that not everything is immediately achievable. By focusing on what *can* be accomplished, she keeps the dialogue positive and open for new ideas to emerge.

- *Am I adding clarity to the discussion?* An old adage claims people need to hear something seven times before it sticks. However, simply repeating information in exactly the same way can make you seem disconnected and condescending. Sometimes reframing, paraphrasing or using different examples can add clarity or help others see things from a different perspective, thus drawing them into the conversation. When you're making presentations or leading a group, reframing or paraphrasing lets you reach a larger audience, since people hear things differently depending on word choice and repetition.

Does It Need to Be Said Now?

Pace is a word used often these days. Deadlines abound. It seems we are all charged with keeping efforts moving faster than ever before. In conversation, you may feel that your thoughts need to be said *right now*. But if you pause . . . to consider the timing . . . you may realize it would be better to wait.

Sometimes the sense of urgency is motivated by fear. You may feel a strong urge to blurt out your idea immediately because "if I don't say this right now, something bad will happen." Learn to recognize when you're being motivated by fear. In my experience, being driven by fear causes irrational conclusions and rash actions. Pausing allows you to sit back and let a conversation unfold, giving all who have an idea the opportunity to share. When I pause, sometimes the conversation goes in a direction where my thought is no longer relevant; other times, my thought is brought forward by someone else in a more appropriate manner; and at times, I share my thought as a part of the conversation, when I get past the fear factor. Again, this creates a safe environment for original thought to come to the forefront.

Another aspect of "Does it need to be said now?" is the golden rule of timeliness: deliver compliments in public and criticism in private. Nothing is sweeter than authentic acknowledgment of a job well done. If there is an audience, they share in the triumph. On the other hand, nothing makes people more uncomfortable than being witness to a public thrashing. No matter how well-intended the criticism, if it is delivered in an open forum, the recipient will find it difficult to feel anything but scolded.

Sometimes a comment may be perfectly logical and current, but you don't have the right audience. Perhaps your thought is around a high-level strategy, but you're sitting with a tactical execution team. Or conversely, while you're in the presence of executive leadership, you may have a thought about how to change a detailed process flow. In either case, the timing is not right. Sharing your idea could slow the momentum for accomplishing the work at hand.

Does It Need to Be Said by Me?

Now, the toughest question: Does it need to be said by me, or would it be better for the message to come from someone else? If what I plan to say reflects *my* feelings and *my* experience, then it will be most authentic when delivered by me.

Going back to compliments and criticisms, beyond timeliness, there is the notion of generosity in leadership. That means giving credit where credit is due. I have learned that personally acknowledging my experience regarding the contributions of others is powerful. It enhances teamwork and mutual respect, and it demonstrates confidence in the leadership abilities of my peers and me. If I am secure in the value I bring to my work, I am not concerned with whether others believe I am the one with all the answers. I can let others' successes take the spotlight. I am not diminished by their success. I look at compliments within a group very simply. When one member of a team wins, it is more likely that she will downplay the success. When two or more win, it becomes a dream team of champions.

Am I the only one with a particular thought or awareness? If so, perhaps it does need to be said by me. It could be that I am the keeper of information to which others are not privy. And if the audience is appropriate, it is mine to share.

However, this guideline comes with a caveat: where possible, avoid name dropping. Consider the following ways to open a conversation:

First: "When our vice president and I were having lunch yesterday, she told me . . ."

Now this: "In thinking about our common goals, perhaps we should consider . . ."

Feel a difference? Uh-huh, I said "feel." This guideline is more about the feeling created through the opening rather than the facts that follow. The first opening positions the listener outside an exclusive conversation. Only the vice president and the speaker were there for this tête-à-tête. The second draws the listener and speaker together. In fact, the speaker actually includes the listener by proxy, using "our."

Also ask yourself, "Will *my* contribution encourage another to share?" There are times when creating a safe environment is not enough to draw out the participation of others. They need to be asked. A directed question can have multiple benefits. It can refocus a conversation that has drifted off track. The response can be the source of new and valuable contributions. The question can also help all parties feel a sense of ownership in the process. All voices have an opportunity to be heard.

Is It Honest and Kind?

The final question is really a gut check: Is what I am about to say honest and kind?

Being *honest* creates transparency and vulnerability. It goes beyond truthfulness. Honesty helps bridge the space between two people by helping each of them better understand what the other is thinking and feeling. I have found it to be essential for any authentic connection.

I've also learned that there are more effective ways to share honestly with someone:

- When sharing difficult information, make sure the environment is "safe"—that is, no distractions or other noise (literal or figurative!).
- Depending on the relationship, it may be helpful for you to ask permission to share your thought, observation, or feedback. The degree of resistance you are met with can help guide you on how, and when, your message is best delivered.
- Speak from your heart—yes, "heart," even when in the workplace. It's okay to share how another's comments or body language made you feel or the impact those comments or actions had. If you are concerned about how your thoughts will be received, seek counsel from a mentor or friend. Someone who is not encumbered by the emotion you're feeling can help coach you on what needs to be said.

Oftentimes, my willingness to take a risk and be vulnerable has resulted in increased honesty from others. They provide clarification on their intent. And the relationship moves forward on new ground.

To the more self-aware and more cordial among us, the inclusion of the tenet of *kindness* may be self-evident. To others, the idea of obligatory niceness may seem gratuitous at best and a pathetic waste of time and energy at worst. Business is business, after all, so why bother? The answer is that kindness makes good business sense. Adversarial communication is not optimal for moving projects, education, or relationships forward. Being kind and courteous is an extension of your respect for another person. If you are having trouble being kind, take a moment to determine what it is that you admire about the person you are working with. I have found that there is always something. In that frame of mind, it's much easier to be kind.

A Matter of Perspective

Taking time to routinely consider these four questions can reorient your perspective. Reflecting on them during conversations may help you recognize the value of diversity of thought and the importance of taking time to understand the strengths of others. You may find you are more effective when you're focused on being of service to others by inviting them into conversations.

Most importantly, being thoughtful with your words frees you up for more listening. Active listeners are engaged and bring richness to a conversation. It often seems that when it comes to communication, there are two kinds of people: talkers and listeners. And while each of us might gravitate to one end of the spectrum or the other, undoubtedly we all benefit from being more discriminating in how and when we engage in conversation.

GETTING NAKED

1. Which of the four questions resonated with you the most and why? How will you incorporate them into your conversations?

2. What other questions or thoughts do you use to determine the value of your communications?

3. How do you draw others into a conversation? What are some of your go-to techniques to engage others' commentary, thoughts, or perspectives?

4. Are you a meeting "stealer"? Do you hog the conversation or berate points made by others? What value is this bringing to the meeting? What will you do differently?

5. Who deserves a compliment from you that you haven't shared yet? Why haven't you shared it? By when will you share this compliment and with what audience?

CHAPTER 11

WHAT IS YOUR LEGACY?

You and a group of your friends decide to go out to dinner, and then comes the dreaded question: "Where do you want to eat?" The hemming and hawing begin, with no one willing to make the final decision. This is a humorous situation we can all relate to, but it illustrates a reluctance to make choices.

There's a story that when Ronald Reagan was a child, an aunt took him to the shoe store to have a pair of custom shoes made. When he was asked whether he wanted round or square-toed shoes, he couldn't make up his mind and told the shoemaker to choose. When he picked up his shoes, one had a square toe and the other was round. He definitely learned to make his own decisions after that!

You have been bombarded with choices every day of your life—what channel to watch, where to go to school, what shoes to wear, which groceries to buy, and so on. Many of these are small choices that are really incidental in your life. However, you must also make serious choices that have a significant impact on your own and others' lives—decisions like where to work, whom to marry, whether and when to have children, how to conduct yourself at work, and what hobbies or passions to pursue. As your choices accumulate, they define who you are and let others see your character and values. The thing is, your career and your life will go more quickly than you realize. Your choices will determine how you live your life, how you spend your time, and what kind of legacy you'll leave.

As a young girl, Vicki wanted to be a beautician. Teachers and guidance counselors told her she was "too smart" and advised her to focus on something more challenging. Reluctantly, Vicki gave up her dream and planned to become a radiologist. Life didn't go according to plan when she got pregnant in high school, got married, and settled into motherhood.

When her mother died suddenly at age fifty-two, Vicki found herself at a crossroads. Should she stay in an abusive marriage and settle for being unhappy and unfulfilled, or take a chance and strike out on her own? She decided to divorce her husband and pursue her dream to go to beauty school. Times were tough for this single mother, but she was determined to build a better life for her children and herself.

After Vicki graduated from beauty school, she began work as a hairdresser. Over time she became a beauty school instructor, a salon manager, and eventually the owner of her own salon and day spa, along with her new husband and love of her life. Together they have built a highly successful business around a cornerstone of taking care of their staff first and creating a safe, happy workplace. Vicki has trained countless staff members from many different backgrounds, with a variety of education, skill levels, personalities, and ages. She provides the support her employees need so they can learn, make mistakes, be accountable, and help the business grow. When you walk into her salon, it's obvious that each person enjoys working there, and it shows in the loyalty of their customers.

Perhaps more important is Vicki's underlying desire to live a life of service, integrity, and purpose. She is driven by her goal to help others feel good about themselves, as well as her belief that the services she provides promote physical and mental health and enable people to be at their best in all parts of their lives. Integrity is woven throughout Vicki's life, and she emphasizes that value with her staff. She's taught countless young people that doing the right thing is the only option, whether that means showing up to work, doing what you say, or offering services to benefit the client rather than one's own paycheck.

And it doesn't stop with her business. Vicki and her husband want to give back to the community they love and that supports them and their business. Over the years they have been involved with Rotary, the chamber of commerce, various hospital and cultural boards, and a host of fundraisers for various charities. They have helped cancer patients deal with changes in their appearance by hosting a free wig bank.

Vicki has devoted considerable time and effort to building her business and a life that she loves. None of this happened by accident. She has made deliberate choices—difficult and painful choices at times—because she wanted something different in her life. And those choices impact not only her and her family, but those she works with. She chooses to believe that her employees do good work, want to contribute their talents, and can be trusted to do the right thing. Rather than letting her time get eaten up by email, meetings, and to-do lists, she chooses to spend her time helping her employees and others be successful.

Not many of us consciously spend time thinking about the legacies we will leave behind. Your legacy is made up of the sum total of the choices you make throughout your life. You create your legacy every day. You learn from your life experiences: the choices you make, how you treat others, the examples you set, and the way you conduct your life. These experiences create your unique legacy.

Vicki's legacy will include what she's taught her children about hard work and doing what's right. It will include the love and memories shared with her grandchildren. It will include the confidence she instilled in cancer patients by providing them with free wigs. It will include her genuine care and concern for her clients' well-being, her terrific sense of humor, her unconditional acceptance of others, and so much more.

Like Vicki, you have an opportunity to begin leaving a legacy today. You do so by how you choose to live and the choices you make. The great thing is that your legacy is not based on your age, your experience, your knowledge, your accomplishments, your income, or how much "stuff" you own. It's based on the way you live. So how do *you* want to be remembered?

Your legacy is the footprint you leave in the lives of others. Picture a quiet beach in the early morning or near sunset and a lone set of footprints headed down the beach. Where are *your* footprints leading? Knowing how you want to be remembered helps you decide how to live and work today.

GETTING NAKED

1. "Legacy" can be defined as the ability to impact others in the future by what you invest today. Are you content with the investment you have made in the lives of people that you lead and those who matter most to you? If yes, why? If not, what will you do differently?

2. What legacy do you want to leave to your family, friends, colleagues, others? Are you living your life to reflect this?

3. If you have children, what will you leave behind in them? How will your life reflect a story they will want to tell their children?

4. Ask several people close to you, "What do you believe my legacy will be?" Another way to ask is, "How would I be remembered if I died today?" Come up with a list of five ways to describe your legacy. Is there anything you want to change about your legacy as it stands today?

CHAPTER 12

LET YOUR BRILLIANCE SHINE

The world craves leadership. Most people do not want to have to think about what to do. Most people are used to being told what do, how to act, and who to be. If we ever hope to be effective leaders of others, we must first be effective leaders of ourselves. In fact, one of the greatest leadership challenges any of us face is the actual act of leading ourselves.

Leading yourself is important because you have a purpose in life—we all do. For example, my purpose is to connect with people on a physical level as a personal trainer and fitness coach. In order to do this at a high level, I can't be mediocre in my own life, living life by default according to what others choose for me. And neither can you.

Fortunately, there are things we can all do to improve our self-leadership. Here are four keys I have found to be helpful.

Develop Self-Discipline

Leading yourself involves self-discipline. Self-discipline is acting according to what you think instead of how you feel in the moment. Sometimes this means sacrificing the pleasure of the moment for what matters most in your life. For example, self-discipline may drive you to go to the gym when what you really want to do is play video games. Or it may get you out of bed early in the morning to study for a needed certification or degree.

There is a quote that says, "We are here to be better than we were yesterday." Your goal is to be better than you were yesterday, to get closer to your optimum self, and to push yourself to your next level, not comparing yourself to anyone else. What you practice day in and day out always pays off in the long run. Think of the stories of Olympic athletes, training day in and day out by themselves, when no one is cheering or even noticing. They do it because they know this is what allows them to be at their best when it counts.

Donna isn't an Olympic athlete, but she's a great example of striving to get closer to her optimum self. She had a two-pack-a-day smoking habit, was seventy pounds overweight, and enjoyed a diet rich in refined, processed foods. She decided something had to change and committed herself to learning what to do to get healthy. She'd be the first to say it has been a long journey, putting one foot in front of the other, experiencing successes and setbacks, and learning to think and act differently. The discipline she has demonstrated to achieve her goals is an inspiration to everyone that knows her. Today she is a successful life coach and a shining example of the benefits of a healthy mindset and lifestyle.

Like Donna, I encourage people to take the drive, courage, and determination they demonstrate in the gym into every aspect of their daily lives. To me, this is what real leaders do. They are the "average Joes" in our community, inspiring everyone they come in contact with by their discipline and enthusiasm. Feeling confident and full of energy is very powerful. It allows people to choose and create the life they truly want—a life they deserve. Life is about living, not just getting through the day. It is about creating . . . living from your desires and your purpose . . . making an impact.

Take Care of Yourself

One of my favorite speakers and authors, Dr. Wayne Dyer, emphasizes the importance of working on yourself each day to bring a sense of peace and balance to your life: "Take time to meditate, practice yoga, read poetry, go for solitary walks, play with children and animals, or do anything that will give you a feeling of loving and being loved." We are all so busy building a career, raising children, running errands, keeping up with friends and family, caring for aging parents, and so much more that it's easy to lose sight of taking care of ourselves.

In order to be at your best, it's important to take of yourself physically, nutritionally, mentally, and spiritually. The more you take care of yourself, the healthier you are and the more you have to give others.

Wayne G. (not to be confused with Dr. Dyer) was only thirty-nine years old, a husband, father, and successful airplane pilot, when he had a heart attack. He learned a hard lesson about the value of regular exercise and good nutrition and what they meant for his ability to be the kind of husband and father he wants to be.

Spiritual and mental aspects of our lives are just as important to overall health. Fill your life with books, music, art, activities, speakers, and friends that motivate you and challenge you to be your best. Use positive affirmations to train your mind to stay positive.

Making the decision to take care of yourself is powerful! I've seen people become better spouses, parents, friends, employees, and employers. They feel confident and empowered. They become more passionate about their jobs. Some people get promotions. Some quit their jobs and start their own businesses. Some decide to no longer settle for mediocrity or a relationship that is no longer serving them.

Dream Big and Set High Goals

Another quote from Dr. Dyer is, "You are not stuck where you are unless you decide to be." What are your goals and dreams, and what are you doing to get there? It's important to get clear about where you are right now and exactly where you want to go, what you want to achieve.

Remember that achieving your goals sometimes takes longer than you want, and you may lose focus along the way. Unfortunately, there is not a dream fairy to dazzle you with a wand and "poof," magically deliver goals and dreams. You will need to get very clear and continue moving in the direction of those goals with focused and directed action.

Adam's dream seemed unattainable to him. At just twenty-six years old, he weighed over three hundred pounds and didn't qualify for life insurance. He just wanted to be healthy and have insurance to protect his wife. He knew he had to make serious changes to his attitudes about food, exercise, and commitment. He broke down his big goal (lose one hundred pounds) into smaller goals and dedicated himself to an exercise routine and improving his nutrition. Commitment is a scary word, but he committed himself to trying things outside of his comfort zone, and it paid off. Not only did he lose a hundred pounds, but he qualified for the premium level of life insurance.

I encourage you to stop playing small. Set big goals and commit to achieving them. You have gifts and talents that deserve to be nurtured. Engage others in supporting you in achieving your goals. Dreams cannot be stopped. Your dreams and desires—no matter how "silly" or "insignificant" they may seem to you—are in need of changing lives, of making an impact.

Help Others Be Their Best

Author John C. Maxwell said, "The point of leading is not to cross the finish line first. It's to take people across the finish line with you." People are already following you, whether you realize it or not. Maybe it's your children, your spouse, friends, or neighbors. Like a drop of water that causes ripples in a pond, each of us impacts the lives of those we come in contact with. Truly inspiring leaders see the best in the people around them and help them see it in themselves. Be aware of the "ripple" you create and decide what kind of impact you want to have. Set an example that encourages others to be their best, that creates space for them to be inspired and to attain their own greatness.

You can start by being your optimum self. It is not selfish—it is essential to your purpose. You must choose to be "all in." Choose to take care of your physical, emotional, and spiritual self. Choose to be your best at all you do—you're going to be here doing it anyway. Be so amazing that others can't look away. Let your brilliance shine—you deserve it! Others are waiting for you to stop playing small, to stop holding back, to show up. They are waiting for you to make a difference—to make an impact. There is nobody in this world who shares your unique, authentic dreams and desires. I believe in you—all you have to do is believe in your authentic dreams. Take time to find out what those really are, and begin moving in the direction to achieve them *now*. When you move with purpose, you collide with destiny.

GETTING NAKED

1. Take some time to quiet your mind, then be honest with yourself as you answer the following questions. Write the answers down before moving on to the next step.

    a. What is your natural gift that others tell you that you have?

    b. If you had three wishes, what would you wish for?

    c. If you had one hour to live, what message would you feel you just had to share?

2. Taking it to the next step . . .

a. Are you contributing your gift in this world? If so, how? If not, what could you do to begin making a contribution?

b. How are you moving toward the manifestation of your three wishes? What is getting in your way?

c. Are you being authentic with your message and sharing it with others? If so, how? If not, how could you be more authentic?

Epilogue

And now you have it—everything you need to know about leading others by being your true, authentic self, summarized in a few short chapters. Ha! Don't we all wish it was that easy? Leadership is a journey similar to living. It takes time and practice, missteps, right steps, and continual humility, because it is more about those we come in contact with than about what we alone can accomplish.

You will note that Naked Feet stories have little to do with one's title or job description. They're more about the impact people have made on others. Whether you are managing employees, influencing work colleagues or your supervisors, or interacting with family, friends, and others who cross your path, you can often find yourself in a position to lead.

Do you know the story of the Velveteen Rabbit, the toy rabbit who eventually becomes real? Similarly, true leaders become leaders over time. Just like life itself, leadership results in bumps, bruises, and moments to be reveled in. The daughter who is charged with settling her parent's estate most likely didn't volunteer for such a task. She may experience a variety of mental and emotional trials as she works through the process, feeling appreciated by some, misunderstood by others. Yet in the end, she may gain a sense of satisfaction, confidence, and self-awareness.

Or consider the highly successful employee who loves his work and is promoted into management, only to discover it's not what he expected and the role isn't fulfilling. When he eventually returns to his previous role, some wonder why he chose to "step down." Others understand that he's following his heart and defining success on his own terms.

These examples and others remind us that somewhere along the line, we all have the potential to start our own journey toward being real. And as we become more real, we continually enhance the quality of our lives and the lives of those around us.

At the start of this book, we said leadership is about becoming your best and inspiring others by how you live, conduct yourself, and interact with those around you. You've now read about real people from all walks of life who made the choice—one step, misstep, or leap at time—to be their best selves. These people weren't born this way; they learned the lessons they needed by practicing the craft called leadership. Publicly leading others by title or position is not for everyone. But we are all leaders in our own lives, whether by choice or not. Maybe by spending a little time with *Naked Feet Leadership*, you've learned some things you want to do differently or validated choices you've already made. Armed with this knowledge, you are, we hope, one step closer to being the kind of leader others want to follow.

To paraphrase a quote often attributed to Hunter S. Thompson, with the addition of our own leadership twist: "Leadership should not be a journey to retirement or the grave with the intention of arriving safely in a pretty and well preserved pair of shoes, but rather to skid in broadside, in a cloud of smoke, thoroughly used up, totally worn out, and loudly proclaiming, "Wow! What a ride we all just had!" May you bring your naked feet self to your leadership style, get real with those you lead, enjoy every mile of your journey, and arrive as a group, sliding in sideways to your finish line!

Acknowledgments

We would like to acknowledge all of the individuals who contributed to this book, whether by letting us tell their story or by being a guest author. If there's one thing we continue to learn, it's that everyone has a story that we can learn from. Thanks to the following individuals for letting us share theirs: Ronnie Blalock Jr., Eli Suggs, Vicki and Tim Tilton, Pamela El, Jim Shasky, Steve Calvery, Kevin Elliott, Jamie Wheeler, and many others who have been the source of valuable lessons in leadership. We also owe a special thanks to our gifted editor, Kathy Carter, and the creative force behind our book cover, Jane Flanders Osborn.

The following individuals agreed to guest author a chapter to share their story in their own words:

SUSAN MITCHELL (Three Cs of Leadership)—Dr. Susan Mitchell is a nationally known speaker and author who focuses on raising healthy, happy families. She has been a family wellness advisor for over two decades and is most recognized for her intensive research on the damage vaccines can cause. She has coached and led thousands of families and doctors alike to live their optimum lives naturally. She is the developer of the website thevoiceforchoice.com, where parents can find information on the many choices in raising healthy families. It is her mission to educate and empower parents across the globe to make informed decisions for their families in all areas of health and wellness. It is her dream that all parents someday will understand that our bodies are designed to heal themselves and that a parent's most important job is to support that process naturally. Dr. Mitchell can be reached at mitchellfamilychiro.com.

ELIZABETH CLARK (Invite Others to the Conversation)— Elizabeth Clark is passionate about her family, her friends, and her career. At any given moment, she is balancing each of these joys with running, reading, art, a cat, a dog, a spiritual journey, giving back, and getting some sleep. She believes every life experience is a lesson if you are willing to be a student. And she is a great fan of words.

JANELLE RAGUSA (Let Your Brilliance Shine)—Janelle Ragusa is an AFAA certified personal trainer, certified CrossFit coach, certified CrossFit Kids coach, and a certified Dr. Sears LEAN coach. She has been in the fitness industry for nearly twenty years. She has taught all types of group fitness and provides one-on-one personal training. She is a member of the McLean County Wellness Coalition and is active on many of the subcommittees as she helps to promote a proactive, healthy lifestyle in her community. She currently focuses on CrossFit and kids' wellness. She works with local preschools to provide physical activity and a nutrition curriculum to enhance the lives of children. Her passion is empowering others to live an optimum lifestyle that is authentic with who they are here to be. You can visit her website at www.fitbodiescrossfit.com or contact her at Fit Bodies CrossFit, 412 Olympia Drive, Bloomington, IL.

And for those of you who want to know more about us, here are some highlights:

Lisa Shasky is an experienced leader, mentor, and communicator who believes every person has unique strengths—the key is identifying them and using the ones that make you happy. Her career has spanned insurance, sales/marketing, banking, risk management, and communications. In her spare time, Lisa enjoys landscaping projects, exercising, and playing with her two cats and three dogs.

Cyndi Streid is a passionate learner, transformational leader, and entrepreneur. She loves to help others learn more about themselves and believes each of us deserves a life we love. Her career has included starting up several companies and departments within the corporate world, as well as her own home rehab business. When not traveling, Cyndi enjoys home remodeling projects and the outdoors.

We can be reached at our website: nakedfeetliving.com.

Other books by these authors:

Naked Feet Living: Finding Your Real Self at Work and in Life

Visit us on our website: nakedfeetliving.com

You can also find us on Facebook/Naked Feet Book Series

www.ingramcontent.com/pod-product-compliance
Lightning Source LLC
Chambersburg PA
CBHW051726170526
45167CB00002B/813